ASHTON-UNDER-LYNE
THEN & NOW
IN COLOUR

DEREK J. SOUTHALL &

GRAHAM S. CHARD

The History Press

First published in 2013

The History Press
The Mill, Brimscombe Port
Stroud, Gloucestershire, GL5 2QG
www.thehistorypress.co.uk

British Library Cataloguing in Publication Data.
A catalogue record for this book is available from the British Library.

ISBN 978 0 7524 8050 3

Typesetting and origination by The History Press
Printed in India.

CONTENTS

ACKNOWLEDGEMENTS

In the course of preparing this book I had many conversations with friends and people who have lived in Ashton all their lives, and I am grateful to them for their patience and for helping me get on the right track. Thanks also to Alan Rose for his knowledge of the Methodist church in Ashton, to Mr and Mrs A. Gill for letting me photograph Trafalgar Square from upstairs in their home in the Twelve Apostles, and Mrs Moreen Butterworth. Thanks also to the managers of the Arcades Shopping Centre and of Ashton Market Hall.

Rob Magee's *A Directory of Ashton Pubs and Their Licensees* was a great help to me in the section of the book which deals with that aspect of Ashton.

The success of a book like this one hinges on the photographic material included. My thanks, therefore, to the *Tameside Reporter* newspaper for letting me use the picture of Mr Whalley's funeral in Trafalgar Square. I am extremely grateful to Alice Locke and her staff at Tameside Local Studies Library and Archive for their patience in dealing with my many enquiries and for finding information which I thought was impossible to find. All of the 'then' pictures were provided by the Local Studies Library and Archive, except nos 5, 18 and 40. Finally, my thanks to Graham, who took almost all of the 'now' pictures. When he agreed to help me with the book I don't think he had any idea what he was letting himself in for. His patience and care – sometimes in conditions which were far from pleasant – were phenomenal, and the contortions he sometimes adopted in order to get the shot he wanted were wonderful to behold. Without him there would be no book!

I have made every effort to ascertain the copyright of the photographs which I have used in the 'then' section. I apologise in advance for any accidental omissions, which I will be pleased to correct in subsequent editions of the book.

Derek J. Southall, 2013

INTRODUCTION

Ashton-under-Lyne is one of the nine towns which make up the metropolitan borough of Tameside, part of Greater Manchester. There is evidence that people have lived in the area for centuries and that it was once mainly a rural area. The name seems to derive from two sources – Ashton from the Old English for 'settlement by the ash trees', and -under-Lyne from either 'lemo' meaning 'elm tree', or 'the line of the Pennines'. In any case, the town is commonly known just as Ashton.

The Industrial Revolution brought a great increase in population to Ashton, along with industry and prosperity. Employment opportunities, both in the cotton mills and the mines, made it an important town. Around the mid-nineteenth century it obtained borough status. The mills – and the employment they brought – declined in the 1930s, but Ashton continued as a major town. In 1973, under the reorganisation of local government, Ashton left Lancashire, to which it had long belonged, to become one of the nine towns which went to make up Tameside; it also became the location of Tameside Council and the borough's administrative centre. Many would say that Ashton is Tameside's main town, but not people from Hyde, Stalybridge and Mossley, among others.

Ashton has been my home since 1959, when I came to the North West from South Wales to take up my first teaching post. Over the fifty-something years I have lived in the town, I have seen many changes, some small, some major. Some of the changes, which have swept away some of the scars of Ashton's industrial past, have made the town a more attractive place to live, though its people remain as warm and friendly as I have always found them.

This book is an attempt to chronicle some of those changes, an effort to ensure that the Ashton of a century ago is not lost forever. I have made every effort to ensure that the facts in the book are accurate, though I should perhaps note that, where facts rely on human memory, discrepancies are not unheard of. It is my hope, and that of Graham, who took the modern pictures, that we have captured in words and photographs some of the changes in Ashton over the years. When I came here to live all those years ago, I thought I would stay two years, before returning to my native Wales. I'm still here in Ashton fifty-four years later – I guess I must like the place!

ASHTON
MARKET GROUND

THIS VIEW OF Ashton market hall and market stalls from the roof of Ashton town hall was taken in the 1950s. Ashton market has been the centre of the town for centuries; a Royal Charter for a market was granted in 1284, and the original market was held in what is now St Michael's Square. The market hall, which was begun in 1829, has been on the present site for almost 200 years. Note how the stalls of the outdoor market begin against the wall of the market hall and are closely packed together. In the background, a bus is passing along Bow Street. To the left of the market hall clock tower can be seen the spire of Albion Congregational Church, and to the right, the tower of the Parish Church of St Michael. The smoke belching from the mill chimneys in the background is indicative of Ashton's industrial past.

THIS VIEW OF the market was taken some sixty-five years later, from the town hall roof on a rainy day. A devastating fire caused much damage to the market hall in 2004. Extensive repairs were carried out, a new roof was added and the market hall reopened in 2008. The two churches are clearly visible in the distance. The market stalls, with their brightly coloured awnings, rather than the drab ones of the original picture, no longer cling to the wall of the market hall and the aisles between them run parallel with Bow Street rather than with the market hall itself. Bow Street is now one way, from Warrington Street towards the market hall; buses no longer use it.

BOW STREET

THIS PHOTOGRAPH, TAKEN from the roof of Ashton market hall, looks over the market stalls towards Bow Street, and dates from the 1940s. On the left is Jones' Music Shop, a popular venue in the 1950s for teenagers to buy or listen to all the latest pop music. Beyond it, past some shops, is the George and Dragon Hotel. The building at the top right of the picture is the *Ashton Reporter* newspaper office. Traffic on Bow Street is one way, with several trolley bus stops fronting the market ground and car parking permitted.

THIS CONTEMPORARY PHOTOGRAPH, taken from almost the same spot on the market hall roof, shows that the block of buildings in which Jones' Music Shop and the George and Dragon stood was replaced by a new block in a 1970's redevelopment. This houses Chris' café, an Iceland store and, in place of the George and Dragon, a club called Oliver's Bar. The Ladysmith Shopping Centre is situated on the far side of Warrington Street and the

Ashton Reporter office was demolished and replaced by a Marks & Spencer store in the 1970s. Traffic, apart from delivery vehicles, is no longer allowed on Bow Street; the trolley buses have long gone.

ASHTON TOWN HALL

ASHTON TOWN HALL from an old postcard, *c.* 1900. The earliest parts of the building date from 1840, though it was extended later. Its impressive frontage, with its Corinthian columns, has dominated the town centre for almost two centuries. Around the time when this photograph was taken, Ashton police station moved from Ashton Baths to a site next door to the town hall. Next to the police station was an inn, and then some houses to the corner with Warrington Street. The market ground on the photograph appears to have been composed of small stone bricks.

THIS PHOTOGRAPH, TAKEN on a spring morning in 2012, shows the town hall and a busy market place. There are now three flag poles, rather than the original one, on top of the building. When Ashton became part of Tameside in 1974, and the town hall was no longer needed as a town hall, it became the site of the Museum of the Manchesters – the Manchester Regiment – and this is reflected in the two cannon on either side at the top of the steps. The police station moved half a century ago and now, to the left of the town hall can be seen the TAC building, Tameside Administrative Centre, added in the 1970s when Ashton became the headquarters of the nine towns which make up Tameside. The market ground is now paved.

ASHTON MARKET GROUND

IN THIS PHOTOGRAPH, which dates from 1936 and which was taken from Warrington Street, we can see Ashton outdoor market ground, with just a few stalls open. In the background is the market hall, and on the left, the town hall and part of the fire station building on Wellington Road. The tram in the centre is on Bow Street, and the tram rails can be seen on Bow Street and on Warrington Street.

THIS CONTEMPORARY PICTURE, taken in summer 2012, shows a very different scene. The market ground is thronged with stalls and shoppers. The market hall, restored and remodelled after a disastrous fire, can be seen in the background and, on the left, behind the trees, the top of the town hall. Bow Street is only used nowadays for market traffic (and bicycles!); the tram lines are long gone and it has been a pedestrianised area for some time.

ASHTON REPORTER NEWSPAPER OFFICE

THE *ASHTON REPORTER* has been, for many years, the town's local newspaper. Published weekly, its distinctive offices were originally on Warrington Street, just beyond its junction with Bow Street. In the photograph the *Reporter* building is decorated for the coronation of Her Majesty Queen Elizabeth II in 1953. The street on the right of the building is Cotton Street. It was possible, when this picture was taken, to look along Cotton Street from Oldham Road and see the Market Hall.

IN THE 1970s much redevelopment took place in the area bordered by Warrington Street, Old Street and Katherine Street. As part of that redevelopment,

the Ladysmith shopping centre was built. The *Reporter* building was demolished
(the offices were moved to Old Street and eventually to Stalybridge); Marks & Spencer
took the site which the *Reporter* had occupied and built their new store, which is shown
in this 2012 photograph. The name of the shopping centre can be seen at the top of the
building to the right of the store. While this book was in preparation more changes have
taken place in the area: Marks & Spencer, having decided to leave the town centre, moved
to an out of town location in January 2013, leaving the building shown here vacant.

ASHTON TRANSPORT BUREAU

ASHTON TRANSPORT BUREAU with buses parked on either side of the building on Katherine Street and Wellington Road, *c.* 1950. The transport bureau, a nicely ornate building, stood on Wellington Road, just across from the market hall. The town hall can be seen in the background; at that time Katherine Street passed in front of the town hall and was the start of several bus routes. The letter H painted on the transport bureau

building is a relic from the war, when it was used to mark the location of a water hydrant. The buses bear the Nos 13 and 45, but they were probably the fleet numbers, since Ashton buses did not have numbers on their destination panels until the late 1950s.

THE TRANSPORT BUREAU was removed many years ago, but the double-decker bus in this contemporary picture is parked on Wellington Road – almost where the bus is in the previous picture. The market hall can be seen on the left, and on the right is the town hall with the open-air market in the centre. Beyond it is the Arcades shopping centre. The picture shows how Katherine Street in front of the town hall is no longer a through way.

ASHTON
FIRE STATION

THIS PHOTOGRAPH OF Ashton fire station, taken in the 1960s, shows the fire station building and, in the distance on the right, the start of Penny Meadow. The street at the back of the fire station is Camp Street, where, at the time, there was two-way traffic, as can be seen from the parked vehicles and the car emerging onto Wellington Road. The fire station opened in 1931 and many who grew up in Ashton will remember the rides which, as youngsters, they were given on the fire engines.

THE OLD FIRE station building remains on Wellington Road, but it has not been used as a fire station for many years since the operation was moved to the West End of Ashton. The building has, since then, been used for a succession of restaurants and pubs, the latest of which is called The Engine Room. As can be seen from the photo, Cordingleys estate agents have offices in the building, as do solicitors Bromley, Hyde & Robinson. Camp Street now exists in name only, since the houses were demolished in the 1970s to make way for the car park which can be seen on the left.

MARKET STREET

THIS PHOTOGRAPH, TAKEN outside one of
the main entrances to Ashton Market Hall,
looks along Market Street towards Henrietta
Street, Cowhill Lane and the bottom of Penny
Meadow. The street on the right, where the
white vehicle is parked outside a shop, is
Fletcher Street. The shop was, for many years,
Burgess and Dyson, Bookseller and Stationer.
Market Street was, at the time this photograph
was taken, a throughway.

THIS MODERN PHOTOGRAPH, taken from
Fletcher Street, shows a very different Market
Street. This area of the town centre has been
redeveloped and opened up. Market Street and
Fletcher Street are traffic free. On the left-hand
side of the picture is the the newly refurbished

market hall. Facing the market hall, across a nicely paved area – which contains a clock with four faces – there is a seating area with an interesting sculpture (seen on the right of the picture) called 'The Family', by Paul Margetts. In the background can be seen the old fire station building, the Ash Tree, and Henrietta Street. The area is now popular with shoppers who want to rest their aching feet (and, unfortunately, with hundreds of pigeons). When the fairground comes to town, it usually occupies the area between Fletcher Street and the market hall.

WHIT WALKS

THE WHIT WALKS, long a tradition in Ashton, see the people of the town's churches walk in procession, accompanied by bands, to the town centre where they meet for a service bearing testimony to their religious faith. In this photograph, from the mid-1930s, the walkers from Ryecroft Independent Chapel are on Wellington Road, just before its junction with Henrietta Street. On the right is the Queen's cinema, showing the Bing Crosby film *Here Is My Heart*. On its left, with a triangular roof, is a snooker hall, and next to that the town's fire station.

IN THIS PICTURE, taken from virtually the same spot in 2012, the Whit Walks are passing in front of the fire station building – no longer the fire station but housing a restaurant, a solicitor's and an estate agent's – and the snooker hall, which is still a snooker hall. The Queen's Cinema, though, has gone, demolished in the late 1950s, and has been replaced by a Wetherspoon's pub, The Ash Tree. The most striking difference between the two pictures, however, is in the onlookers. In the 1930s the Whit Walks were an event which brought crowds out in Ashton, with people lining the streets four or five deep (as in the first picture) to watch the procession, which took an hour or more to pass on its way to and from the market ground where a religious service was held. In 2012 there is only a scattering of spectators, mainly people who are in Ashton to shop; the service is no longer held on the market ground but on a back street car park. The second picture is startling evidence of the waning of religious faith over the past century.

VANISHED ASHTON

THIS PHOTOGRAPH FEATURES an
apparently nondescript car park in
central Ashton, yet behind it is a
poignant story. The street at the top of the
picture is Warrington Street; the one on
the right-hand side is Wellington Road.
The triangle of land within those streets
originally held three streets, of which only the
roads remain in this picture – Tatton Street
(nearest the camera), Jermyn Street and
Gosford Street. Those three streets of terraced
houses were home to dozens of families,
a community within a community – some of
the people who gave the town its heart.
When this picture was taken, the streets
had been swept away, the families dispersed,
the community broken up. Why?

THIS PHOTOGRAPH, TAKEN in 2013, provides the answer. The camera looks from the bottom of Penny Meadow, along Wellington Road to its junction with Warrington Street. On the left hand side is the back of Ashton town hall and beyond it the huge building known as TAC – Tameside Administrative Centre. This building stands where hundreds of people once lived, where Tatton Street, Jermyn Street and Gosford Street once stood. The TAC was built when Ashton became the main town of the new Tameside Metropolitan Borough. The three streets were demolished to make way for this enormous building – people replaced by concrete! The different departments of the council are in TAC and the ground-floor space is shared with a Wilkinson's store. Ironically, as this book is in preparation, there are reports that Tameside Council is planning to have TAC demolished and a smaller headquarters built in a different part of Ashton. In a book devoted to changes in places and buildings, these pictures are perhaps most important for the social significance of their back story.

ASHTON CHARLESTOWN RAILWAY STATION

THE STATION WAS opened in the early years of railways by the Ashton, Stalybridge and Liverpool Junction Railway, which later became part of the London, Midland and Scottish Railway. It provided a train service on the trans-Pennine route between Manchester and Yorkshire. This photograph, *c.* 1960, shows the station with two entrances – a side entrance and the main entrance. The street to the right of the station is Sackville Street.

THIS UNUSUAL AND unique view of Ashton station was taken in July 2012. The crowds outside the station, whose name can be glimpsed on the left, are welcoming the Olympic torch to Ashton on its journey around Britain before the start of the 2012 Olympic Games – proof, if any were needed, of the popularity of the Games. The second moldern photograph is of Ashton station (note that the Charlestown name

has been dropped) in 2013. The frontage is much changed and the side entrance has gone. In 2012 the car park was extended, and now passengers exit the station onto the rather grandiloquently named Ashton northern bypass. This new road, built (according to rumour) at a cost of some £15 million to relieve traffic congestion on Penny Meadow, takes vehicles to/from the traffic lights outside the Prince of Orange along the line of the railway, across Henrietta Street and Cowhill Lane from/to the top of Penny Meadow. Sackville Street was swallowed up in this bypass.

HENRIETTA STREET BRIDGE

THIS PHOTOGRAPH, TAKEN from the railway bridge on Henrietta Street in the 1980s, looks across to Suffolk Street and Camp Street and, on the right, down to the bottom of Henrietta Street, where it joins Penny Meadow. It shows a densely populated area of Ashton, the houses huddled close together, and one of the many corner shops that were familiar in every town like Ashton. The tower of the parish church is just visible above the rooftops on the right-hand side.

THIS PHOTOGRAPH, TAKEN from almost the same location, shows a very different aspect. The closely packed houses in their mean streets have vanished; demolished in the aftermath of the formation of Tameside. It's hard to escape the thought that people were cleared out of the centre of Ashton in the 1970s to let the motor car in! The tower of the parish church and the spire of the Albion Congregational Church are now clearly visible. The road crossing the scene from right to left just below the railway bridge is Ashton's newest road, the northern bypass. Opened in January 2012, this stretch of road, constructed at a huge cost and with much disruption, is very short – it starts at Charlestown Station and ends at the top of Penny Meadow. Yet it brought another set of traffic lights to Henrietta Street, and cut the bottom end of Cowhill Lane off from the rest of the lane.

29

CAMP STREET FROM HENRIETTA STREET

THIS PHOTOGRAPH, TAKEN in the 1970s and looking in the opposite direction to the preceding one, shows Camp Street, looking from Henrietta Street to Wellingon Road. Camp Street once ran from Cowhill Lane to Wellington Road on either side of Henrietta Street. This section had business premises on the left-hand side and dwellings on the right. The road in the foreground is Henrietta Street.

FOUR DECADES LATER, the landscape in this part of Ashton is much changed. The dwellings on Camp Street have vanished, compulsorily purchased and demolished in the 1970s with the birth of Tameside. The huge, ugly building just to the left of centre is the administrative centre, which was required for the new metropolitan borough. Car parking space was required for the centre and Camp Street, along with the parallel Suffolk Street, was consigned to oblivion and replaced by the vast car park, seen on the right of this photo, and replicated on the other side of Henrietta Street. The Camp Street name alone still remains and traffic is now one-way along the street from Wellington Road to Henrietta Street. The car parks have recently been diminished by Ashton's northern bypass, the road marked in the photograph by the sign on the right-hand side.

PENNY MEADOW

THIS VIEW OF Penny Meadow more than a century ago was taken from the junction of Henrietta Street and Wellington Road, looking up Penny Meadow. It was then – as now – a busy street, thronged with people visiting the shops. Apart from the horse-drawn cart, the picture is remarkable for the absence of traffic, as well as for people standing or walking in the middle of the road. The building on the right is the Bowling Green Hotel, opened in 1792 as The Hare and Hounds. It became the Bowling Green in 1805.

THIS VIEW, TAKEN from just outside Ashton market hall on a spring morning in 2013, looks up Penny Meadow towards the building which was originally Albion Schools (centre right of the street). The building on the extreme left of the picture is a Wetherspoon's pub, and next to it, at the corner of Henrietta Street, the Kwik Fit premises. On the opposite corner of Henrietta Street are premises that were occupied for many years by Howarth's, a popular confectioner's. They are now the offices of New Charter, a very visible presence in Ashton. Beyond them is Cowhill Lane and Westhead's Florists. As it was a century ago, the Bowling Green Hotel, albeit more strikingly coloured, is still prominent (the second building from the right). Penny Meadow, despite all the traffic changes wrought in the centre of Ashton, and although the nature of its shops have changed greatly from a century ago, is still a busy part of the own and one of the area which gives Ashton its character.

STAMFORD STREET FROM THE MEMORIAL GARDENS

THIS PICTURE, FROM the Memorial Gardens on Cricket's Lane, dates from the 1960s. It shows houses and some shops on Stamford Street, between St Michael's Square and Albion Congregational Church. St Michael's Square is centre right. Dominating the

skyline is the tower of the Parish Church
of St Michael and All Angels, which
dates from the fifteenth century, although
there is evidence in Domesday Book of a
St Michael's Church in the area before the
Norman Conquest.

IN THE 1960S this part of Ashton was
drastically and dramatically changed.
A triangular built-up area including
England Street, bordered by Scotland Street,
Bedford Street and part of Stamford Street,
was demolished to make way for a huge
roundabout, onto which converge roads
from Ashton, Mossley, Stalybridge and
Dukinfield. Situated on this roundabout was
a new telephone exchange, the huge building
centre left of this photograph. The roads in
the picture are the four-lane carriageway
of the roundabout, with the junction with
Cricket's Lane on the right. Though there is
little traffic in the picture, the roundabout
is used by thousands of vehicles every day.
Still clearly visible, though perhaps no longer
dominant, is the tower of the parish church.

STAMFORD STREET

FOR MANY YEARS Stamford Street was
Ashton's main shopping street. Beginning
in Chester Square, it ran all the way
to Stalybridge. The section from Henry Square
to St Michael's Square provided the town's
central shopping area. Two-way traffic on
Stamford Street made the street so busy in
the mid-twentieth century that the pedestrian
crossings had to be manned by policemen.
The centrepiece of Stamford Street and the
most popular store in the town was Arcadia,
the Ashton Co-operative department
store, situated between Oldham Road and
Cavendish Street. This photograph, from early
in the twentieth century, shows the section
of Stamford Street from Cavendish Street to
Henry Square. There are shops on both sides
and beyond them can be seen the tower and
the building of Ashton Baths and, in the
background, the tower of St Peter's Church.

WHEN PLANNING PERMISSION was given in the 1970s for the Ladysmith
shopping centre – then the Arcades – in the area bordered by Katherine Street, Old Street,
Warrington Street and Delamere Street, the death knell sounded for Stamford Street,
and ultimately for Arcadia. The store remained open until 1993, and after its closure, stood
empty for more than five years. Then the whole block, including the Spread Eagle public
house which adjoined Arcadia, was sold to the German business, Lidl. The new owners
decided that the Arcadia building did not suit their needs, and had the building demolished
and a new store built, which is seen here centre right beyond the cars. Next right,
beyond Lidl, is Ashton Primary Care Centre, built just a few years ago in the area bounded
by Old Street, Henry Square, Stamford Street and Cavendish Street. Just beyond the building
on the left stands a huge traffic roundabout, part of the town's southern bypass. The most
distinctive buildings remaining from the first picture are the buildings of Ashton Baths –
still there, though sadly neglected – and the tower of St Peter's Church.

OLD STREET

HERE WE SEE a section of Old Street – from the junction with Cavendish Street to Henry Square – as it was for many years. We are looking west, towards St Peter's church, its tower just visible to the left of the 'no left turn' sign. Two very popular Ashton shops can be seen on the left of the picture – Ashton Models, which specialised in all kinds of model aeroplanes, ships, cars etc. and Bride-To-Be, which speaks for itself. Beyond them, the tower of the old Ashton Baths in Henry Square is visible. The building on the right-hand side of the street is the Witchwood (formerly known as the Globe Hotel), a popular live music venue.

TWENTY YEARS ON the whole aspect of Old Street has dramatically changed. Most of the original buildings have gone and almost all of the street from Cavendish Street to Henry Square is occupied by Ashton Primary Care Centre. It is the relentlessly modern building on the left, which is, however much it boasts to have been 'two years in the planning' and to 'promote sustainable technologies, 'rainwater harvesting systems' and 'roof-mounted solar panels', some might say, rather boring and characterless. Tameside Centre for Enterprise, a similar building, is on the opposite side of Old Street. One of the few distinctive buildings to still survive in this part of the street, adding some character to this part of Ashton, is the Witchwood public house, seen clearly here on the right-hand side of the picture).

HENRY
SQUARE

THIS 1950s PHOTO of Henry Square, taken from outside Ashton Baths, shows the junction of Stamford Street and Old Street, two of Ashton's busiest thoroughfares at the time. Both were two-way and the striking aspect of the photo is the sheer volume

of traffic, merging from three directions. Stamford Street, then Ashton's main street, was thronged with shops and with people from Henry Square to St Michael's Square. The Friendship Inn is the building on the extreme left.

THIS IS ONE of the most changed areas of Ashton. It is now called St Petersfield and is the home of the new magistrates' court (seen on left). Old Street and Stamford Street still come together here, but the volume of traffic is very much lighter and there is no access here from one to the other. The southern bypass takes through traffic, while traffic for the central market area and for Oldham now uses Katherine Street. Stamford Street is no longer a throughway. The large white building which has replaced Shipley's Tours is part of Tameside and Glossop Primary Care. Ashton Baths, long derelict, but protected, can still be seen on the right, and the Friendship Inn, though closed, is still there.

VIEW FROM HENRY SQUARE TO CHESTER SQUARE

IN THIS PHOTOGRAPH, dating from around 1900, we are looking west from Henry Square towards Chester Square. The main street is Stamford Street and the woman in the foreground is standing on the corner of Welbeck Street. Beyond the

houses is Chester Square, and in the distance, the imposing St Peter's Church. The tram in the square and the tram lines show the route of trams to and from Manchester.

A PHOTOGRAPH TAKEN from almost the same spot as the previous one in 2013 shows that the houses on this part of Stamford Street and Welbeck Street have gone – demolished in the redevelopment of this part of Ashton. St Peter's Church still stands beyond Chester Square, and has given its name to this part of Ashton, which is now called St Petersfield. The busy road on the left of the picture is Ashton's southern bypass, which takes traffic round the edge of the town from Chester Square to St Michael's Square. The block of flats on the extreme left is Ryecroft House. The sculpture, centre left, marks a terrible tragedy in June 1917, when there was a tremendous explosion in Ashton's West End. Forty-six people died – many of them children on their way home from school – and more than 400 were injured. The munitions explosion also made hundreds of people homeless. The sculpture, designed with much help from children at St Peter's Primary School, remembers all those killed, injured and made homeless by that explosion.

43

WELBECK STREET

THIS RATHER BLEAK photograph looks from the
bottom of Welbeck Street towards Henry Square.
The block of flats in the background is Welbeck House,
and the black car is just leaving Henry Square.
The building with the tower is Henry Square Methodist
church; the shop is on the corner of Church Street,
and the building between Church Street and Park Street
is St Peter's Church of England School, which was a
century old at the time of the photograph.

WELBECK HOUSE CAN still be seen in this
contemporary view from roughly the same location.
Henry Square Methodist was closed and pulled
down in the 1960s when the church merged with
Trafalgar Square Methodist church to form West End
Methodist, which still stands on Trafalgar Square.
The school was also demolished, and St Peter's Church
of England Junior School is now in the West End of
Ashton. The road along which cars are travelling
in both directions is Ashton's southern bypass from
St Michael's Square to Chester Square, which follows

what used to be Park Street and Park Parade. Ashton baths, with its tower, can be seen on the right – closed and derelict, but a listed building, so protected. The one new building prominent in Henry Square is seen behind the trees in the centre – Tameside Magistrates' Court, part of the redevelopment known as St Petersfield.

OLD STREET AND PORTLAND STREET SOUTH

THIS PHOTOGRAPH SHOWS just one corner of Henry Square, where Portland Street South and Old Street emerge into the Square. The buildings just inside the square include a couple of cafés and a Jet petrol station. For many years Henry Square would

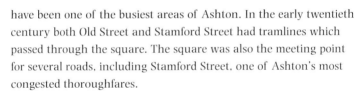

have been one of the busiest areas of Ashton. In the early twentieth century both Old Street and Stamford Street had tramlines which passed through the square. The square was also the meeting point for several roads, including Stamford Street, one of Ashton's most congested thoroughfares.

A NEW CENTURY and a new Henry Square – at least in this corner. The imposing building which dominates the north side of Henry Square, replacing the cafés and petrol station, is Tameside Magistrates Court. Part of Ashton's St Petersfield project, it is one of the town's most impressive modern buildings, which people like to admire as long as they don't end up there! The tower of St Peter's church is seen in the distance – a neat juxtaposition of religion and justice. In the foreground, on the far right is the Friendship Inn – long a feature of this part of Ashton, but now closed and up for sale. The square, once busy and noisy with traffic and people, is today a quiet area, an open space where Ashton's citizens can walk, sit and relax, and, if they choose, meditate upon the nature of justice!

VIEW FROM
THE TOP OF
HILLGATE STREET

HILLGATE WAS ONCE an area of closely packed terraced houses, with poor amenities, its streets narrow, steep and congested. This photograph, taken some fifty years ago from the top of Hillgate Street, looks down to the new housing being built to replace those demolished terraces. The public house on the left at the bottom of Hillgate Street is the Seven Stars.

THIS RECENT VIEW from the same location shows the housing on the hill long since completed. On the right-hand side of Hillgate Street the properties – many of them old and run down – have been replaced by the Ashton Central Mosque, which was built in 2010 and dominates the area, making a striking contrast with the opposite side of the street. The Seven Stars public house can still be glimpsed at the bottom left of Hillgate Street but, since the picture was taken, it has been demolished.

JUNCTION OF OLDHAM ROAD AND WELLINGTON ROAD

THIS PHOTOGRAPH SHOWS the LMWR railway yard and weighbridge which occupied a large site at the corner of Oldham Road and Wellington Road for the greater part of the twentieth century. The site was eventually taken over by Norweb (North Western Electricity Board) which had its offices there for many years. When Norweb was swallowed up by North West Water to form United Utilities in 1995, the offices in Ashton were closed and demolished and the site sold.

TAKEN FROM THE same spot in 2012, this photograph shows the IKEA store, which opened in 2006 on the railway yard site. One of the largest, most distinctive (if not aesthetically pleasing) and most controversial buildings in Ashton, this IKEA store, which can be seen from many miles away in all directions, was the first to open on a town centre site. The Oldham Road and Wellington Road junction is now one of the busiest in the town. The rail in the foreground is part of the Metrolink tram system. After what seems like years of disruption to Ashton roads and traffic, it is due in 2014.

OLDHAM ROAD
AND TAUNTON ROAD

THIS VIEW, LOOKING north, shows the junction of Oldham Road and Taunton Road as it appeared in the first decade of the twentieth century. The buildings on the junction itself are the buildings of Christ Church Schools. The church is hidden behind the schools. On the right of the picture is the Hop Pole public house with its tower; the pub has occupied this site since 1882. Note the interweaving tram lines and the carts pulled by horses – on the wrong side of the road!

A CENTURY LATER and Oldham Road is a main thoroughfare, carrying large volumes of traffic from Ashton to Oldham, Rochdale and the north. Christ Church Schools are long gone, demolished in the 1940s, and the Hop Pole public house still occupies its prominent site at the corner of Cranbrook Street and Oldham Road, though it is now closed and for sale. The houses on the left are on Taunton Road, where there has been much building since the original picture was taken.

CURRIER LANE AND SCOTLAND STREET

CURRIER LANE, WHICH connects Ashton with Stalybridge, emerges onto Scotland Street. In the centre of this photograph, taken late in the 1960s, we can see some common lodging houses and shops on Scotland Street. Common lodging house is a Victorian term for a sort of cheap accommodation in which many people, from various families, are lodged together. The tower in the background is the tower of St Michael's parish church. The building on the right is the Blue Bell public house, on that site since 1881.

THIS CONTEMPORARY PICTURE shows that the common lodging houses and the Blue Bell public house are long gone; the line of cars waiting to enter the roundabout bears witness to the fact that the

'Telephone Exchange Roundabout', at the eastern end of Ashton's southern bypass, is now a prominent feature of this part of Ashton. The only surviving link with the previous picture is the magnificent edifice of St Michael's parish church, which has dominated this area since the fifteenth century, though much of the church was rebuilt in Victorian times. What changes St Michael has witnessed!

ASHTON
POLICE
STATION

AT THE BEGINNING of the twentieth century Ashton's police station was in Ashton Baths. It was later moved to the town centre next to the town hall. When, in the 1960s, a decision was taken to move out of town, a new police headquarters was built on Manchester Road, opposite St Peter's church and between Manchester Road and Jowetts Walk. In this picture, taken soon after the new police station's opening in 1963, a lowering sky looks down on Ashton. The block of flats in the background is Welbeck House, and the trolley bus wires above the road show that trolley buses were still in use in the 1960s.

IN 2012 WE see a new police station, the smart and brightly coloured building which replaced the one in the first photograph in November 2004. Welbeck House can just be seen against the skyline to the right of the photograph. Manchester Road, originally two lanes each way in front of the police station, is now four lanes and one way, creating, with Stockport Road, the traffic island on which St Peter's Church is now marooned.

HURST CROSS
IN THE 1950s

HURST, ORIGINALLY A
village about a mile away
from the centre of Ashton, is
today a suburb of the town.
Its centre is Hurst Cross,
where King's Road,
Queen's Road and
Lees New Road come together.
The present cross was
constructed with funds
raised by the people of Hurst
Village to commemorate
the Reform Bill of 1867,
which enfranchised many
working class men for the
first time. This photograph
of Hurst Cross, taken in
the 1950s, shows the cross
prominent in the foreground,
with shops and derelict

houses on the left of the photograph. The public house – the white building in the centre of the picture – is the Royal Oak, at the corner of Nook Lane, and, just beyond it, Lees Road begins its long journey to Oldham.

THIS CONTEMPORARY PHOTOGRAPH, taken from a slightly different perspective, keeps Hurst Cross in the foreground with the public house and Lees Road background centre. The major innovation in the photograph is Hurst Library, the modern building to the left of the Cross, which replaced the shops and derelict houses, and which was opened in November 1987 by local MP Robert (now Sir Robert) Sheldon to replace the very small library on Queen's Road. Unfortunately, not fifteen years later, the local council, claiming that it has to make cuts in its expenditure, has felt it necessary – in spite of strong local opposition – to close this much-loved library along with four others in the borough and put the building up for sale.

THE TWELVE APOSTLES

THIS ROW OF houses in Trafalgar Square, in the West End of Ashton, was built in the 1860s by local mill owner and philanthropist Hugh Mason. Intended for the foremen of his two local cotton mills and their families, it has always been, and still is – a century and a half later – known locally as the Twelve Apostles. The petrol lorry, which can be seen centre, is fuelling the petrol station which stood, somewhat incongruously, on a site in front of the Twelve Apostles for a time.

OVER 150 YEARS after they were built, the Twelve Apostles attest to the skill and solidarity with which they were constructed. Over the past sixty years the properties have been put to many uses. For long periods they have been neglected and have given the appearance – graffiti, broken windows and doors – of a slum property. A few years ago the terrace was taken over by a housing trust, and the houses restored to their original glory inside and out. The petrol station is long gone. This photograph, taken on a sunny day in spring 2013, shows Hugh Mason's statue – which now has its home in Trafalgar Square – very appropriately facing the Twelve Apostles, which he had built across the square. Anyone entering or leaving Ashton by way of Stockport Road cannot fail to notice the Twelve Apostles, one of Ashton's most distinctive buildings.

ASHTON CANAL AND
PORTLAND BASIN

THIS VIEW OF the Ashton Canal, taken from a bridge over the water, looks towards the derelict Junction Mill, built between 1831 and 1890. This cotton-spinning mill ceased business in 1930. The mill's chimney, central in the picture, octagonal in shape and 201ft high, was built in 1867. The bridge on the left crosses the Peak Forest Canal, which connects with the Ashton Canal at this junction, where the Peak Forest Canal, the Ashton Canal and the Huddersfield Narrow Canal meet.

THIS PHOTOGRAPH, TAKEN from the same bridge, shows part of what is now known locally as Portland Basin Heritage Centre. Junction Mill is long gone, but its distinctive chimney still dominates the view. On the right of the picture, smart new apartment blocks have replaced the mill. The quay, centre right, fronts the Portland Basin Museum, a popular tourist attraction, which is housed in the former Ashton Canal warehouse. The canal is now mainly used for leisure activities, including fishing – fishermen can be seen on the left below the bridge. The barge approaching the bridge is *Zenith No 2*.

CAVENDISH MILL

CAVENDISH MILL, ALMOST 130 years old, is a reminder of Ashton's prosperous past as a cotton-spinning town. The mill was built alongside the Ashton Canal, beside Cavendish Street, by Potts, Pickup & Dixon, for the Cavendish Spinning Co. between 1884 and 1885 and has, since then, been a feature of the canal bank.

CAVENDISH MILL CEASED to be a cotton spinning mill in 1934, but the building, one of the few mill buildings which survive in the town, was put to a variety of uses over the next sixty years until, in 1994, it became a resource centre for the community, as well as containing commercial units and 165 apartments. It is also the home of Tameside Community Radio. This photograph, taken from the canal footpath, shows the building as it is today, part of a pleasing amenity area along the canal. In the background can be seen the Asda superstore and the tower of Ashton parish church.

PROPOSED
UNITARIAN CHURCH

A CENTURY AGO Katherine Street extended from Hardwick Street, on Ashton Moss,
all the way to the bottom of Penny Meadow, passing in front of the town hall. Near its
western end it is bisected by Richmond Street. It was at this junction of Katherine Street

and Richmond Street that the Unitarian Church chose a site for their new chapel at the start of the twentieth century. The foundation stone of the proposed chapel, shown in this diagram, was laid in April 1906 and the completed chapel was opened in April 1907.

THIS PICTURE SHOWS the junction of Katherine Street and Richmond Street just over a century later. The Unitarians worshipped in their church on the site until July 1983, when the final service was held there. In 1985 the building was sold to the Muslim community, which used it as a place of worship until 1999. The building was then demolished and work started on a new mosque. The Masjid Hamza Mosque, which took several years to complete, is now one of the most striking and distinctive buildings in modern-day Ashton, and one of the first buildings which visitors see on entering the town from the west.

ASHTON MOSS COLLIERY
(SNIPE COLLIERY)

THE AREA ALONG Manchester Road, just before the boundary with Audenshaw, was once occupied by one of several Ashton collieries. The Ashton Moss Colliery (often referred to locally as the Snipe Colliery, perhaps because of the closeness of the

Snipe Inn) opened in 1875, when the demand for coal was growing rapidly. In 1882 a second shaft was sunk to a depth of 2,850ft, the deepest in the world at the time. The colliery dominated and scarred the landscape, while providing much employment in the area for almost a century.

THE AREA PRESENTS a very different aspect today. The Ashton Moss Colliery has gone, closed in 1959, despite the fact that it employed some 500 men and was producing 150,000 tons of coal a year. Today the site is wholly occupied by the Snipe Retail Park (as can be seen on the road sign), accommodating B&Q, Curry's and several other large retail stores. Much of the land is occupied by car parks and the retail park itself, as it is a magnet for people at the weekends.

THE WORKHOUSE

THIS POSTCARD FROM 1910 shows Ashton Workhouse. The purpose of a workhouse was to 'offer accommodation and employment to those who were otherwise unable to support themselves.' A workhouse had first been established on Dungeon Street (now Market Street) in Ashton town centre in 1729. More than a century later the building seen in this picture was erected on land adjoining what is now Fountain Street; it could accommodate 500 inmates. A hospital block was added in 1866.

A NEW INFIRMARY was built in Ashton in 1906, and in 1948, when the NHS was formed, that infirmary and the old workhouse building became Ashton General Hospital. Over the years the hospital has undergone great expansion, not least in the last few years. This picture was taken on Fountain Street, looking towards the A&E Department and the new buildings which house wards, clinics and X-ray facilities. Since 1976 and the formation of Tameside the hospital has been known as Tameside General, and serves the nine towns of Tameside as well as Glossop. A Foundation Trust hospital since 2008, it seems to be continually bedevilled by controversy and bad headlines.

ELGIN STREET INFANTS SCHOOL

ELGIN STREET INFANTS School – seen here on an old postcard – opened in 1910, when its headmistress was Miss B. Whitworth. For some sixty years, through two world wars – in fact boys from the school would have fought in the Second World War – the school remained a formidable presence there on Elgin Street. Successive generations of pupils would have seen much development and many changes in the local landscape.

THIS MODERN PRIMARY school, also on Elgin Street, is the successor to the Elgin Street Infants School. The modern school is a bright, open building, a startling contrast with the tall, dark, threatening Victorian school. The present school opened on 6 April 1970, with pupils from the Elgin Street Infants School and Christ Church Gatefield Infants School (which had opened in 1863). The new school was named after Canon Alan Douglas Johnson, who was born in 1883. He had served as a chaplain in the First World War, when he was awarded the Military Cross. He also served in the Second World War. He remained a bachelor, and he devoted much time to the five schools connected with Christ Church. He never lived to see his dream of a new primary school on Elgin Street come to fruition, since he died suddenly in 1957. It is fitting that the school which he visualised should have been named after him.

HURST JUNIOR AND HURST COUNTY INFANTS SCHOOLS

OLDHAM WHITTAKER, A mill owner in Ashton in the mid-nineteenth century, was responsible for much building in the Hurst area of the town, especially along Queen's Road. Among his buildings was a school, Hurst Junior School, on Queen's Road between Whiteacre Road and Alderley Street (shown in the first picture). Although most of the trustees were Methodists, and the building was both a day school and a Sunday school, it was open to children of all denominations and hence was known as 'Hurst Undenominational'. Also, because of its brickwork, it was known to all as 'The Black School'. The building opened on Christmas Day 1858, and the first pupils entered on 1 January 1859. Fifty-two years later, Ashton council built a new infants' school, Hurst County Infants School, just across Alderley Street from the junior school (second picture). This building, of Accrington brick, was known locally as 'The Red School'.

THE BLACK AND the Red Schools stood side by side on Queen's Road
for some sixty-three years until, in January 1974, the Black School,
ravaged by fire, was rendered unusable. The local authority, which was
by then involved in the running of the school, erected some temporary
classrooms at a Methodist Primary School on Lees Road to help out. What
remained of the Black School was demolished and new houses now occupy
the site. Nearly thirty years later, the Methodist Church decided to build a
new primary school for the pupils from both the Red School and from the
school on Lees Road, which would be demolished. The new school was built
on land owned by the Church at Higher Hurst alongside Rosehill Road,
land once occupied by the pay corps attached to Ashton barracks.
The new school, Rosehill Methodist Community Primary School, opened
in September 2003 in low, modern, airy and exceedingly well-protected
buildings, and has flourished ever since. A Sure Start Children's Centre
is attached to the building. Over 150 years on, though the location has
changed, the tradition of education in Hurst continues.

ASHTON GRAMMAR SCHOOL

THIS PHOTOGRAPH SHOWS part of Ashton Grammar School in the 1950s. It was founded on Old Street as the Ashton-under-Lyne Secondary Day School and Pupil Teachers' Centre in 1904. By the 1920s new premises were being sought and when space was found alongside Darnton Road, it was decided to build a new school there. The new school opened in 1928 and from then on was called Ashton-under-Lyne Grammar School, eventually a co-educational school for pupils aged eleven to eighteen.

SINCE 1972 ASHTON has been one of the nine towns which make up the Metropolitan borough of Tameside. In the late 1970s, after a battle over education which went to the House of Lords, Tameside Council implemented a scheme for comprehensive education in the borough, under which Ashton Grammar School became one of two sixth form colleges (the other was Hyde Grammar School). In 1992, under the Further and Higher Education Act, sixth form colleges, which had been under LEA control since secondary school reorganisation, became independent. This view of Ashton Sixth Form College, taken from Arundel Street, shows that the college has undergone considerable expansion, the original building being seen between two very recent additions. The college is a thriving and very successful establishment, and still a landmark on Darnton Road in its eighty-fourth year.

THE PITT
AND NELSON
PUBLIC HOUSE

TRADITION HAS IT that the Pitt & Nelson dates back to the late seventeenth century. The pub occupied a prime site in the town centre, where Old Street, Market Street and George Street meet. In his book, *A Directory of Ashton Pubs*, Rob Magee notes that the

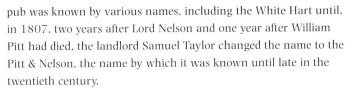

pub was known by various names, including the White Hart until, in 1807, two years after Lord Nelson and one year after William Pitt had died, the landlord Samuel Taylor changed the name to the Pitt & Nelson, the name by which it was known until late in the twentieth century.

DURING ITS LONG lifetime of nearly 250 years as a public house, the Pitt & Nelson had many owners and landlords and many names as a public house. Its final incarnation, the Pitt & Nelson, was the name that lasted the longest. Towards the end of the twentieth century, as fashions changed and old-style pubs were no longer 'in', many closed or were converted to gastropubs. The Pitt & Nelson was among the former, closing in 1989. The building, however, survived, reopening briefly in various guises, among them a short-lived nightclub called the Bedroom. In 2013, the building, distinctive as ever, houses a food store called 'DJ's discount foods'. The shop on the corner, which was for many years occupied by Harold Schollar & Son, Butcher, now houses a computer repair business known as Sana Tech.

YATES'S WINE LODGE

YATES'S WINE LODGES were a chain of public houses, founded in Oldham in 1884 by two Preston brothers, Peter and Simon Yates. The houses were mainly in the north of England, though there were a few in the south. The chain opened a new house in Ashton not long after the business began, in a prime location on Old Square,

Stamford Street, which was at that time Ashton's main and busiest thoroughfare. A large and impressive, if dour, building, Yates's Wine Lodge dominated Old Square for more than 100 years, though the centre of Ashton was moved from Stamford Street to the outdoor market area in the 1970s.

TOWARDS THE END of the twentieth century Yates's Wine Lodges, like many other pub chains, saw their trade decrease considerably. After various changes of ownership, the chain was taken over in 2005 by the Laurel Pub Co. Though the new owners refurbished some of their premises, they put the Ashton building up for sale. It reopened as a club called Legends, but that was short-lived and quickly closed. Empty and forlorn for some time, it has recently been taken over by the Pet Man, a familiar name of long standing on Stamford Street. After running his business for many years on the opposite corner of Old Square from the Wine Lodge (as can be clearly seen in this contemporary photograph), his sign now stands proudly where once the Yates's logo dominated.

THE NEW NOOK

IN THE 1870s a beer tavern in
Ashton bore the name the Old Nook.
Owned privately until the 1930s, it
was then purchased by Gartside's
Brewery. Seven years after the end of
the Second World War the license was
transferred to a new establishment,
which was mooted for Lees Road
in Ashton, at the junction of
Broadoak Road and Lees New Road.
That new pub did not open until
the autumn of 1958 and, naturally
enough, was called the New Nook.
From its opening the building was
a prominent landmark at that busy
road junction.

THE NEW NOOK had a facelift and
a change of name in the 1990s,
when it became the Turnpike,
named after the location of a

turnpike nearby many years before. In 2012 it underwent not only a name change but also a change of function. Closed for some months for refurbishment inside and out, it reopened as an Indian restaurant, the Amaani – a sign of changing times and changing cultures.

GAUMONT CINEMA

THIS PICTURE'S CENTREPIECE is Ashton's Gaumont cinema, opened in 1920 as the Majestic; the year is probably 1945, since *Up in Arms*, released in August 1944, would have taken several months to reach Ashton. The picture's most striking feature is the long queue, stretching back along Old Street almost as far as Warrington Street, as well as down the other side of the cinema towards Stamford Street. The queue on one side was probably for the stalls, the other side for the more expensive seats in the circle, as was usual in those heady days of cinema. Such queues were a very familiar sight at that time, when cinema was a cheap and very accessible way of getting away from the stress of life in wartime. The nurses at the entrance are probably St John Ambulance nurses. Older, somewhat ramshackle buildings next door to the cinema house some shops.

THE BUILDING WHICH housed the Majestic (later the Gaumont) cinema is still on Old Street. The cinema, absorbed into the J. Arthur Rank set-up in the mid-1940s as the Gaumont, retained that name until November 1962, when Rank renamed

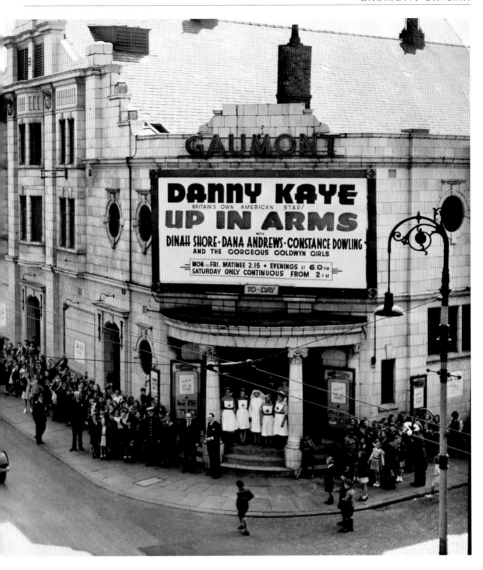

it the Odeon. Its central position made it a very popular entertainment venue but, when audiences began to dwindle, Rank sold it to a local independent cinema owner. Operating as the Metro cinema from November 1981, it lasted until September 2003 when the opening of the Cineworld fourteen-screen multiplex out of town precipitated its closure. The building later operated as a slot machine arcade, Slotworld (just what Ashton needed!) until it closed in 2011 and was boarded up. The old buildings adjacent to it have gone, replaced by the local Trustee Savings Bank (TSB). A striking difference between the two pictures is that, in the 'then' picture, just one car is visible, coming along Old Street from Warrington Street. A 'now' picture without several cars in the frame was impossible – a sign of how, in some seventy years, the car has taken over people's lives.

PAVILION CINEMA

THIS PHOTOGRAPH, TAKEN on Old Street, probably in 1960 – the Pavilion's advertised film *Sink the Bismarck!* was released in that year – shows the library in the distance, a row of shops outside which the van is parked, the Pavilion cinema and the Salvation Army hall. The cinema opened just before Christmas 1908 as the Picture Pavilion. The owner, William Henry Broadhead, had given Ashtonians a brand new entertainment house, with 1,600 seats, while silent cinema was still at its height. Always a popular venue, the Picture Pavilion never belonged to either of the major cinema circuits – Rank or ABC. It had its share of publicity – film star Anna Neagle visited in the late 1930s – and it brought a major cinema innovation to Ashton when the first CinemaScope film, *The Robe*, opened there in 1954.

THIS CONTEMPORARY PHOTOGRAPH shows that the Pavilion building remains on Old Street more than a century after the original cinema opened. After the cinema's closure in 1966, it operated as a bingo club for the next thirty-four years; first Cosmo, then Gala. In 2000 Gala moved to new premises on Wellington Road and the building stood empty until it was sold a few years ago to new owners, who are furniture retailers. As Pavilion Furniture it at least retains its cinema name, and is still a prominent landmark on Old Street. The interior of the building has hardly altered and for cinema-goers, evokes memories of the wide auditorium and the screen space across which sprawled the vast expanse of the CinemaScope screen. The owners also bought the Salvation Army hall next door, the wall of which carries their logo. Beyond the Pavilion building there is still a row of (very different) shops and the library can still be seen in the distance.

THE ROXY CINEMA, HURST CROSS

A FEW YARDS from Hurst Cross, the Roxy cinema (seen in this photograph across Queen's Road from Whittaker Street) opened in December 1938. In the photograph, dating from the 1960s, we see the Roxy when it had become a bingo club. As a cinema its first film was the popular Deanna Durbin musical *Three Smart Girls*. Owned by a Mr Joe Gomersall, the Roxy was a landmark in the Hurst area. The cinema frontage, as can be seen from the picture, was very impressive. Cinema-goers entered a nicely decorated foyer, then the cinema stalls. There was no balcony. Instead, the floor at the rear of the stalls rose sharply, to provide a 'balcony' area, for which prices were higher. The cinema, somewhat unusually, changed its programme every two days, usually showing films which had already been seen in Ashton's central cinemas. The author visited the Roxy in 1959 and remembers that the curtains, which masked the screen, did not quite meet at the bottom.

THIS PICTURE, TAKEN from Old Lees Street in 2013, shows that the Roxy building, a fixture at Hurst Cross for sixty years, has vanished and been replaced by an Asda superstore, set further back from Queen's Road. The original houses of Whittaker Street and Old Lees Street were demolished, and only the name of Whittaker Street remains, though Old Lees Street has new dwellings on it. The Roxy continued as a cinema until July of 1960, when falling attendances forced it to close, as many suburban cinemas did around that time. It became the Roxy Bingo Hall, continuing as such until the late 1970s, when that too closed. The building was then sold, and, with the auditorium gutted, became the premises of Quilting Ltd. That company was succeeded by Palm Beach Clothing, but, by the end of the century, the old Roxy was boarded up and derelict. Early in the new century the building was demolished and the land sold for a superstore. The Co-op was its first owner, but they closed it in 2009. Sold again, it is now the premises of the Asda superstore.

ODEON
GUIDE BRIDGE

IN THE YEARS before the Second World War, with the advent of sound in film, cinemas proliferated in the north-west. Seen in this photograph, dating from the late 1930s, is one of the most splendid – the Odeon, Guide Bridge, opened in 1936. Built as the Verona, it was taken over by Odeon shortly before it opened. A luxury cinema, the finest in Ashton (just on the boundary between Ashton and Audenshaw), it had seats for more than 1,100 customers and very quickly established itself as a popular venue for a night out. It is easy to understand from this picture why a night at the Odeon was an exciting prospect in those golden years of cinema.

THIS 2012 PHOTOGRAPH makes a sad contrast to the previous one – perhaps, for lovers of cinema, the saddest in this book. The Rank Organisation decided to close some of its cinemas in 1961, and the Odeon was among the victims, closing in March of that year. The building was bought by the Catholic Church and, for some forty years, was St Paul's Roman Catholic church. When the diocese decided that the church was no longer viable, it was closed and put up for sale or to let, which explains its rather run down appearance in this contemporary photograph.

EMPIRE
THEATRE

THIS PHOTOGRAPH, DATING from around 1910, shows the Ashton Empire and Hippodrome Theatre in its early days. The theatre opened as part of the Broadhead Circuit in 1904. The frontage was plain red brick. There was a shop on each side of the entrance. The seating capacity, with stalls, circle and boxes was 2,000, and it quickly established itself as a popular entertainment venue.

MORE THAN A century later the building remains on Oldham Road, shuttered and run-down, but still there after a chequered career. In 1933, when sound had come to cinema and picture houses were flourishing, it became a cinema and, after a few months, part of the Union circuit. A year later ABC took it over, operating it until 1964, when they sold it to EMI. Eleven years later it was taken over by Tameside Council which operated it as a theatre, with films in the summer, but in 1983 leased it to Apollo Leisure. Apollo transferred it to Live Nation and in 2008, after a dispute with the council, Live Nation bowed out. The council declared the theatre needed a lot of work which they could not afford, and closed it. Widespread opinion was that they would sell it and shops, flats or similar would be built there, but in 2012 a group formed to save the theatre appears to have gained the council's blessing and there are hopes that it will reopen as a working theatre in 2013.

TRAFALGAR SQUARE
IN ASHTON'S WEST END

TRAFALGAR SQUARE, IN the west end of Ashton,
lies alongside Stockport Road, one of the main roads
out of the town towards the west. The subject of the
first picture, taken in 1958 and reproduced courtesy
of the *Ashton Reporter* newspaper, is the funeral of
Bert Whalley, coach to Manchester United, who was
killed in the Munich air crash. Stockport Road
runs through the picture; the hoardings are
at the beginning of Hamilton Street and the
streets running parallel with Stockport Road
are Kelvin Street and Fitzroy Street. The large
buildings on the right-hand side are the
church and Sunday school of Trafalgar Square
Methodist church, where Mr Whalley and
his family worshipped. The second picture,
taken in 1962, is a closer view of those buildings,
and the Sunday school has gone, replaced by a
different single-storey building which was the new
Sunday school, opened in that year. To the right
of that new building can be seen the corner of
Trafalgar Square Day School.

THIS PHOTOGRAPH OF the north side of Trafalgar Square, taken in February 2013, shows that this side of the square has undergone a dramatic transformation. The large old Methodist church on the corner of the square has vanished, demolished in the 1960s after falling victim to dry rot. The building on the extreme left replaced it, but became the Sunday school when the Church Council decided to continue using the building next to it as the church. By that time it was West End Methodist church, an amalgamation of the old Trafalgar Square and Henry Square Methodist churches. The building to the right of the church, which replaced the day school, is St Peter's Children's Centre and Children 4 Most day centre, built in the early years of the twenty-first century under the Sure Start project. The statue of Hugh Mason stands proudly in the centre of the square. Behind the church and children's centre can be seen the new houses of Fitzroy Street, built when the area was redeveloped in the first decade of the twenty-first century.

If you enjoyed this book, you may also be interested in…

Voices of Oldham
DEREK J. SOUTHALL

The sense of community was very strong and this book records the stories and reminiscences of over thirty Oldhamers, in their own words. Their vivid voices recall childhood games, work, shops and entertainment, as well as the effects of war and bombing raids. This book is illustrated with a wealth of photographs from the personal collections of the interviewees, adding considerably to the power of their stories and making this an important social and historical document as well as a fascinating read.

978 0 7524 3544 2

From Balti Pies to the Biggest Prize: 'The Transformation of Manchester City
STEVE MINGLE

From Balti Pies to The Biggest Prize relives the journey from perpetual also-rans to champions, from laughing stocks to a team to be feared, fuelled by the injection of unimaginable finance. The money has changed the calibre of the team on the field but how much has it changed its fanbase, its culture, its soul? Steve Mingle's book gives a unique perspective on exactly how it feels to be City today.

978 0 7524 9320 6

The Golden Years of Manchester's Picture Houses: Memorie of the Silver Screen 1900-1970
DEREK J. SOUTHALL

This is a delightful collection of memories from the golden age of cinema in Manchester. Filled with archive images, it recalls courting days and war-time air raids, the stars, the staff and all the magic of the silver screen.

978 0 7524 4981 4

Visit our website and discover thousands of other History Press books.

www.thehistorypress.co.uk